TOTALLY WEIRD

Night Animals

Contents

Glad to eat... I mean, MEET you.

Tricky words are explained on page 32.

Midnight world

When night falls, most animals curl up and go to sleep. But many nocturnal, or night, animals are just waking up. Leaves rustle and mysterious shapes haunt the shadows, as these moon-loving creatures begin a busy night.

That's weird

Nocturnal animals have a special kind of clock inside their bodies. At dusk, it sounds an alarm, which wakes up the snoozing creatures and brings them out of hiding. Then, at dawn, another alarm sounds and they go back to bed.

Turning detective

Most night animals disappear into the shadows before you see them. But you can use crafty sleuthing skills to unmask them. Look out for tell-tale clues left behind, including footprints and tracks, loose feathers, clumps of fur, scraps of food and even droppings!

That's not my cat!

Dodging dinosaurs

The first night animals appeared on Earth millions of years ago, during the time of the dinosaurs. These shrew-like creatures scuttled out at night while the dinos slept. This way, they could hunt for food in peace.

▲ Cats spring into action in the dark. At night, these eagle-eyed creatures hunt for food, play, fight and mate, while other animals are sound asleep.

What do cats read to catch up with the news? A newspaper!

HA HA!

Eye spy

Night animals don't miss a thing in the dark! Many of these sharp-eyed creatures have huge, bulging eyes to let in as much light as possible. Others peer out through thousands of miniature eyes.

Yikes!

Magical mirrors

Is it a ghost? No, it's just a pair of cat's eyes, shining in the beam of a torch. A layer at the back of each eye reflects the light like a mirror and helps the cat to see in the dark. Big cats in the wild also have eyes that work like mirrors.

▲ A tarsier's saucer-like eyes make the most of the dim light. Even when a tarsier is taking a nap, it keeps one eye open for danger.

Open-and-shut case

A gecko licks its eyes to keep them clean! During the day, a gecko protects its sensitive eyes by narrowing the pupils to leave just thin, dark slits. This shuts out most of the blinding sunlight. At night, when the gecko is busy hunting for its dinner, the pupils open wide.

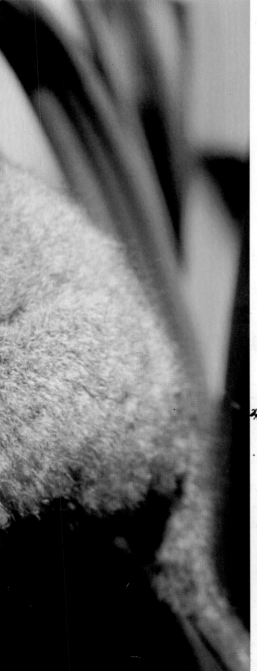

Two-tone vision

Imagine watching a TV with the colour switched off! Anteaters and most other night animals are colour blind, which means they see only in black and white. Also, everything looks blurred, so it helps that they have a good sense of smell and hearing.

Under the microscope

A mosquito is a night-time nibbler that can see in all directions at once. Each eye is made up of thousands of tiny six-sided eyes, which let the mosquito see pictures in many parts, just like a mosaic.

Music to their ears

The night is full of strange noises, from ringing chirps to eerie howls. To us, it means nothing, but to other animals, these sounds are warnings, invitations or just ways to say hello!

honk

honk

Nice song, shame about the face.

What's in a name?

Ha ha

Ha ha
Ha ha

A hyena splits its sides laughing at the sight of a few tasty bones! This cackling creature earns its name from the howling laughter it makes after a successful hunt. When other members of the pack hear the calls, they join the feast.

Beastly suitors

A hammerhead bat is no Prince Charming. Its lips are huge and its cheeks bulge out. But what it lacks in looks, it makes up for in song. Groups of males hang upside down from trees, making ear-splitting honking sounds to attract females. When a female flies past the ugly line-up, she picks the loudest male.

Dangerous call

A male cricket has to pick its partner carefully. It finds a mate by making shrill chirping noises. But the calls also attract the sneaky tachinid fly, which lays eggs on the cricket's body. When the eggs hatch, the young flies eat the cricket.

▲ The chilling howl of a coyote warns other coyotes to keep away.

In spring, the night air around ponds and swamps is thick with croaks, grunts, squeals and whistles. It's the breeding season and romantic male frogs are in fine voice, trying to attract mates.

Hello, gorgeous!

The calls guide female frogs to the breeding place and warn rival males to keep their distance. For the females, it's love at first sight and sound — they hop off towards the croakers of their choice.

Tuning in

Most night animals have an excellent sense of hearing. This helps them to hunt for food, avoid the clutches of predators and find their way around in the darkness.

Night-time rustles

A serval on the prowl keeps its ears pricked, listening out for tasty treats. The merest rustle of a juicy mouse sends this wildcat plunging through the long African grass in hot pursuit.

GETTING AN EARFUL!

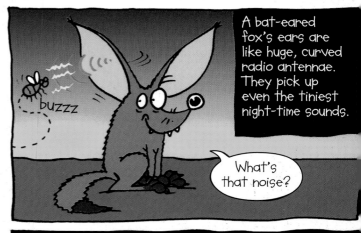

A bat-eared fox's ears are like huge, curved radio antennae. They pick up even the tiniest night-time sounds.

What's that noise?

buzzz

The flexible ears can turn up, down, left, right and even in two different directions at once!

It's enough to tie your ears in knots.

buzzz

stomp

The fox uses its ears to pinpoint termites, its favourite food. The fox can even hear them in their holes underground.

Sounds like dinner.

stomp   stomp

Strange but true

When an aye-aye hears a grub, it bites right through the tree bark. Then it scoops out the struggling insect with its long middle finger.

Who are you calling big ears?

Clickety-click

An oilbird has a special way of avoiding bumps in the night. It makes clicking sounds as it flies. These sounds bounce off trees in its path and return to the bird. By listening to the echoes, this tropical bird judges how close objects are and how to avoid them.

Home, sweet home.

Totally batty

All day long, snoozing bats hang around in caves, trees and attics. But when dusk falls, these airborne acrobats take to the night sky, fluttering their leathery wings.

Hey, move over!

Hook, line and sinker

A fishing bat is an expert night-time hunter. This fierce fighter grabs prize catches from rivers and lakes. The secret of its success is echolocation. The bat makes short, sharp shrieks and listens for the echoes that bounce back off ripples made by fish in the water. Then, it drags its feet through the water until it hooks its slippery prey.

Crowded quarters

Bats live in groups called colonies and often sleep thousands to a roof! A cave in New Mexico, USA, is home to a vast colony of more than 20 million bats. During the day they rest, hanging upside down by their hooked feet.

BAT VERSUS MOTH

Bats love to hunt moths. But the tiger moth knows how to fight back. First, it loops and dives like mad.

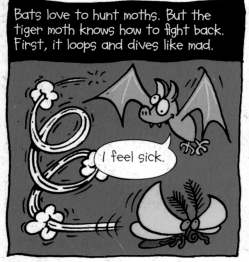

I feel sick.

If that fails, the moth makes a loud popping sound. This can startle the bat so much that it gives up the chase.

POP

Was that you?

As a last resort, the moth folds its wings and plummets to the ground. Then it hides until the bat clears off.

Where did he go?

Strange but true

A bat gives an insect a big hug before eating it! The bat sweeps its wings around the crunchy snack and guides the prey into its open jaws.

Grub's up!

▲ A furry Californian leaf-nosed bat swoops towards its dinner. The bat's wings are made of skin stretched over long, thin fingers, just like the fabric covering the frame of an umbrella.

Sniffing it out

Many night animals have an unbeatable sense of smell, with nifty noses for sniffing out food. Often, these animals give off smells, too — either to frighten off enemies or to attract mates.

▲ A kiwi is one of only a few birds that can smell. At night, it probes the forest floor with its long, thin bill, sniffing out worms, beetles and other tasty titbits.

That's weird

A female emperor moth attracts a mate by giving off a strong scent that wafts on the night breeze. A male moth's super-sensitive feathery feelers, called antennae, can pick up the enchanting scent from over 11 kilometres. That's more than 100 football pitches laid end-to-end.

My sweetheart!

Homing in

A storm petrel would be lost without its trusty sense of smell. This nocturnal sea bird lives in a huge colony of birds and has to find its own nest in the dark. Luckily, it has an excellent nose for the smell of its own bedding.

To the rescue...

Follow your nose

Fierce South American army ants hunt mainly at night. Up to half a million ants march along the forest floor, following the scent trails of other ants in the colony. When an ant is attacked, it releases an odour that works like an alarm, calling for more reinforcements.

Bottoms up!

Mess with a night-feeding skunk at your own peril. This smelly creature sends predators packing by sticking its bottom into the air and firing off a foul spray. The dreadful stench clings to fur for weeks – if you're unlucky enough to be downwind of this stinker, the smell will make your nose wrinkle almost three kilometres away!

Night hunters

Night animals have clever ways to catch their midnight snacks, including lying in wait and setting sneaky traps.

Dawn raid

Cunning foxes, stripy badgers and masked raccoons can't resist a night-time meal of yummy leftovers. These furry thieves sneak into gardens and alleyways while you're asleep. They search for tasty pickings in dustbins and rubbish dumps. Then, before dawn, they scurry off with their haul.

Success story

Ha! Didn't take long to track you down!

A pit viper uses a dastardly secret weapon to spot a tasty frog hiding in the dark. Two sneaky little holes beneath the snake's eyes sense the warmth given off by the frog's body. What a warm glow!

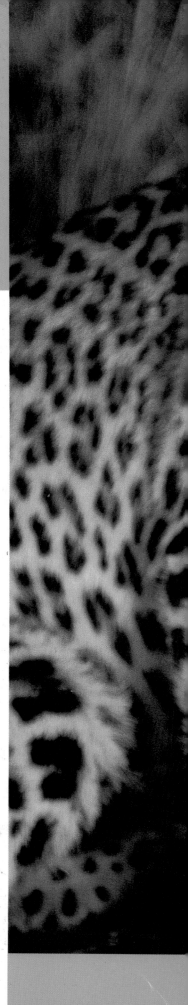

Gulp!

Hairy antics

A scorpion is a nocturnal hairy hazard. When an insect buzzes by, tiny warning bristles on the scorpion's body vibrate. The scorpion quickly grabs the insect with its pincers and stings it with its poisonous tail. Ouch!

Strange but true

A leopard pulls prey equal to its own weight up into the trees with its teeth! Here, its catch is safe from thieving hyenas.

Net trick

A net-throwing spider spends its evenings patiently sitting on a branch. First, it spins a web, which it stretches over its front legs. Then, it waits until an insect walks underneath and drops the net, trapping the creature below.

▲ A leopard crouches in the undergrowth, ready to pounce on its prey. Its spotted coat helps it to blend into the night.

Phantoms
of the
night

Few animals are more at home in the dark than owls. These ghostly birds are deadly hunters, with super-sharp eyesight and long-range hearing.

IT'S A HOOT

Cough mixture

Owls eat first and think later! They wolf down mice, voles and other small prey without chewing. But they're not so keen on bones, fur or feathers. So after a while, they cough up the offending bits, bundled into dark pellets.

That's weird

An owl is an amazing contortionist. It can twist its head around to face backwards and even upside-down. When an owl is trying to track down a juicy snack, this acrobatic skill is extremely useful!

Whoo hooo!

Winged phantom

People tell creepy stories of ghostly shapes flitting across moonlit churchyards. The culprits are usually owls which sometimes glow in the dark. The glow is given off by luminous fungi that catch in an owl's feathers after it has rubbed against damp tree bark.

Believe it or not

A barn owl has such fine-tuned hearing that, even high in the air, it can pick up the squeaks and scuffles of mice hidden beneath snow.

▲ This barn owl is swooping silently towards its victim. The owl's feathers are soft, with a fluffy fringe to muffle the sound of its flapping wings.

Family matters

Nocturnal families get together under cover of darkness. Parents have babies and search for new homes, while youngsters play with each other and learn about growing up.

MONSTER EGGS

A nocturnal kiwi lays a jumbo-sized egg. She waddles around for several nights before finally squeezing it out.

Phew! What a whopper! I'm finished.

The male kiwi takes on the tricky job of keeping the huge egg warm until it hatches. This can take up to 85 nights!

This isn't very eggs-citing.

When the chick hatches, it's fully feathered and raring to go. Many other baby birds begin life blind and bare.

I wish I had feathers like that.

Foxy fun and frolics

When young foxes play, it's a mini battlefield. Every evening, these rowdy youngsters, called pups, burst out of their hole to play. Under the watchful eye of their mother, the pups learn vital hunting skills. They play-fight with each other and pounce on anything that moves, from crackling leaves to their parents' tails. Sometimes, an adult throws the pups a live mouse to tease and bully!

▼ At night, opossum babies travel in style, taking a trip on their mother's back. As many as seven tiny passengers can pile on to the mum-mobile!

All aboard!

Fishing lessons

Young raccoons are butterfingers. A mother raccoon teaches her young to feel for fish with their fingers in the moonlit water. At first, they are too excited to net a catch, but soon they become handy hunters.

That's weird

A shrew leads her young family on a night-time search for a new nest. Together, they look like a line of conga dancers. Each baby shrew holds on with its teeth to the bottom of the brother or sister in front.

Olé, Olé!

Glowing in the dark

In many parts of the world, eerie lights flicker and twinkle in the night sky. The dancing flashes are beamed out by glow-worms and fireflies. It's a bright way to get a message across in the darkness!

That's weird

In the past, people in South America trapped fireflies in containers and used them in their homes as living light bulbs. They also tied fireflies to their ankles when walking at night.

Flashy flies

In Southeast Asia, male fireflies turn trees into huge torches that can be seen for miles around. Thousands of the fiery insects gather in the trees. Their bodies flash on and off to attract female fireflies.

Home visit

The brightly lit body of a fungus gnat lures night-flying insects into caves. The insects then become trapped in long, sticky threads that the gnat has spun from the roof of the cave. The crafty gnat, glowing with pride, hauls up its dinner, like a fisherman reeling in a catch.

Put me down!

Lure of the lights

A firefly attracts a partner with romantic lighting. Each type of firefly has its own pattern of flashes, which it sends out like a message in Morse code. A female firefly waits until she recognizes a pattern before flashing back a welcoming message in reply.

You're cute!

Fatal attraction

The female *Photuris* firefly is a deadly copycat. She imitates the light signals of the smaller, harmless *Photinus* firefly to lure the little males to her side. The unsuspecting fireflies land eagerly beside the hefty impostor, only to be swiftly grabbed and eaten.

Pleased to eat... I mean, MEET you.

Believe it or not

Glow-worms are not really worms at all. They are the larvae, or young, of firefly beetles.

▲ Most glow-worms beam out light from their behinds. They use special chemicals to produce the flashes.

Daytime hangouts

During the day, night animals usually keep a low profile. They hide away in cool places, safe from predators. But a few bold creatures sleep out in the open, craftily disguised so they can't be spotted.

Stumped for success

When it comes to acting, a frogmouth is a really wooden performer. This nocturnal flier spends the daylight hours impersonating a broken tree branch. The bird's dull brown feathers and lack of movement are a convincing act.

Let sleeping cats lie

Lions are active at night, but pass the daytime hours fearlessly lounging about in the shade. They rest for up to 20 hours at a stretch. These big cats have no need to find a safe hideaway because no other creature is foolish enough to attack them.

Shhh.

Sleepy hide-outs

Honduran white bats snooze the day away under a tent made from large leaves. After a hard night's hunting, they hang upside down, clutching the main vein of a leaf with their clawed feet.

"Where's my sleeping bag?"

▲ During the day, a pangolin curls up in its burrow. A predator needs teeth of steel to bite through the pangolin's scaly armour.

Tell me why

HIPPOS ARE COOL CUSTOMERS

Yippee!

At night, hippos are out and about. But during the hot day, they chill out by wallowing in mud and splashing around in rivers. This lazy pastime helps to protect their skin, which burns easily in the sun.

Phew.

Hippos have another clever way of keeping cool in the heat of the day. Their skin oozes a reddy-pink, oily liquid to stop it from drying out. In the past, this led people to believe that hippos sweated blood!

Desert life

Most desert animals prefer the night shift, when the hot daytime sun has gone down. They are shade-loving beasts, custom-built to make the most of life among the sand dunes.

What's in a name?

When is a fish not a fish? When it's a sandfish! This scaly lizard moves across the dunes at dusk and dawn, wriggling like a fish. To escape the jaws of an attacker, it snaps off its tail and dives headfirst into the sand.

Not again!

I'm out of here!

BOING

Success story

A jerboa is totally unsinkable! At dusk, this sand-dweller pops out of its burrow to feed. It has large toes, which spread out wide to stop it from sinking into the sand. At the first sign of trouble, the beast bounds away like a kangaroo, covering the length of a small car in a single leap.

Clash of the titans

In the ring with a scorpion, a camel-spider is a champion fighter. This nasty night-time spider grows to the size of a saucer, or about 15 centimetres from one leg to another! It dances around the snappy scorpion like a boxer, before leaping in and chewing off the scorpion's poisonous sting.

I win!

24

Believe it or not

During the day, a fennec fox's big ears help it to survive in the hot desert. Heat escapes through the giant ears, helping the fox to cool down.

▲ During the cold desert nights, a fennec fox feels the benefit of a thick fur coat. The fox also has long fur on the soles of its feet to keep it warm and to help it trot easily over the hot sand.

Ocean world

The oceans swarm with creatures on the move. At night, many of them hunt for food and lay their eggs in the murky waters. In the blackest depths, strange fish never see the light of day.

Believe it or not

Many deep-sea fish are real bright sparks. They make their own light inside their bodies so they can find their way in the dark.

▲ This scary-looking marine monster is an anglerfish. It has a glowing fin on its back, which it wiggles about like a fishing rod to lure small fish. Then it snaps up the victims in one big bite.

Night-time garden

A coral reef is not just a pretty sight in the ocean waters. Each coral is made up of thousands of tiny animals called polyps. At night, the corals wave and fan out their spindly tentacles to attract tiny swimming animals into their mouths.

A gulper eel is all mouth. This slack-jawed deep-sea horror swims through the black waters with its jaws wide open, scooping up anything that swims by. After a big dinner, its stomach bulges out like a balloon.

Watery eggs-plosion

For one night only, a grunion is a seaside star. Once a year, on a moonlit night, millions of these tiny fish leap out of the water. They wriggle into the sand to lay their eggs. Then they dash back to the sea, unless a flocking sea bird gobbles them up first.

Ocean archer

A Portuguese man-of-war never misses its target! This ghostly night-feeder waits for a fish to wander into its trailing tentacles. Then it grabs the fish with its tentacles and fires off a harpoon-like dart. Finally, it reels in its prey on the end of the harpoon.

A viperfish also swims in the dark with its huge jaws open. But it goes one better than a gulper eel. This fish's mouth is lined with long teeth for stabbing its victims. The fiendish fangs curve inwards to stop its prey from escaping.

Night-time nightmares

It's spooky in the dark! The strange goings-on of night animals have led to many terrifying tales of make-believe creatures, from swamp monsters to werewolves.

WHO TURNED OFF THE LIGHTS?

Ghastly guzzler

The make-believe stories of Count Dracula are based on the behaviour of real-life vampire bats. These fierce-looking animals sink their razor-sharp fangs into sleeping animals to suck their blood!

SUCKER FOR BLOOD

Dracula is the spine-chilling star of horror stories. At night, the fanged fiend wakes up to guzzle human blood.

Where did I put my fangs?

Quick as a flash, Drac changes into a vampire bat. Then he swoops out of his creepy castle to find a victim.

This is no time to hang around.

When Dracula is about to pounce, he drops his bat disguise. Now, only a cross can scare him off!

Fangs for having me.

Creature from the black lagoon

Australian legends tell of a blood-curdling, swamp-living monster of the night, called the bunyip. It is said to have flippers like a seal, tusks like a walrus, and a head the shape of an emu. It also has a deafening roar and a taste for human flesh. Yikes!

29

Night champions

Amazing records abound in the nocturnal world, from aerial acrobats and deafening music-makers to bristly beasts and the ultimate lazy-bones.

Geronimo!

Watch out – it's a flying squirrel! These super-stylish gliders launch themselves off trees at night. Flaps of skin stretch out from the squirrel's arms and legs like wings, turning it into a daredevil hang glider. A flying squirrel would have no problem covering the length of a football pitch in one swoop. Whoosh!

Wonder wings

The Bismark fruit bat is one of the biggest bats of all. This shadowy creature of the night measures a truly terrifying 1.8 metres from wingtip to wingtip. That's almost twice the width of your outstretched arms!

Hello there!

Sharp warning

A North American porcupine bristles with as many as 30,000 spines, making it the prickliest night animal. When this living pin-cushion is threatened, it rattles its quills in warning. As a last resort, it lashes out with its tail, leaving hundreds of quills stuck in its enemy's skin. Ouch!

Ow! That hurts.

Night song

In many hot countries, the night air rings with the sound of bush crickets. These champion chirpers are among the world's loudest insects. Even if you were sitting in the front of a long train, you could hear a bush cricket chirp from the back end!

SHUT UP!

Slow motion

Yawn! There's no hurrying a sloth. This sleepy-head is one of the world's laziest animals. It snoozes for days on end, hanging securely from a branch by its hook-like claws. When a sloth does stir itself, it crawls incredibly slowly on its belly – standing up takes too much effort! It creeps along at such a snail's pace that moss has time to grow in its hair.

Index

Author: Iqbal Hussain
Illustrations: Gary Boller
Consultant: Jonathan Elphick
Photographs: cover: SuperStock; Tony Stone Images (background); p3: Bruce Coleman Ltd; p5 (top): Robert Harding; p5 (bottom): Science Photo Library; p7: NHPA; p8: Planet Earth Pictures; p9: Minden Pictures; p11: Oxford Scientific Films; p12: PowerStock/Zefa; p13: FLPA; p14/15: Tony Stone Images; p17: Planet Earth Pictures; p18: Oxford Scientific Films; p19: NHPA; p20: NHPA; p21: Bruce Coleman Ltd; p22: Oxford Scientific Films; p22/23: Bruce Coleman Ltd; p25: Telegraph Colour Library; p26: Planet Earth Pictures; p27: Oxford Scientific Films; p28: Fogden Natural History Photographs; p29: Hammer Film Productions, courtesy of the Kobal Collection; p30: Oxford Scientific Films; p31: Images Colour Library.
Every effort has been made to contact the copyright owner of the image of the tarsier monkey reproduced on page 4/5. Two-Can hopes to be able to correct this omission in future editions of the book.

Published by Two-Can Publishing, a division of Zenith Entertainment plc, 43-45 Dorset Street, London W1H 4AB

Created by act-two, 346 Old Street, London EC1V 9RB

ISBN: 1-85434-794-2
Dewey Decimal Classification 591.51
A catalogue record for this book is available from the British Library.

Paperback 10 9 8 7 6 5 4 3 2 1

Printed in Hong Kong by Wing King Tong